W9-AUW-205

The Wonders of our World

Rivers & Lakes

Neil Morris

CRABTREE PUBLISHING COMPANY

The Wonders of our World

Crabtree Publishing Company

350 Fifth Avenue,
Suite 3308
New York,
New York 10118

360 York Road, R.R. 4
Niagara-on-the-Lake
Ontario
Canada LOS 1JO

73 Lime Walk
Headington
Oxford
England OX3 7AD

Author: Neil Morris
Managing Editor: Jackie Fortey
Editors: Penny Clarke & Greg Nickles
Designer: Richard Rowan
Art Director: Chris Legee
Picture Research: Robert Francis

Picture Credits:
Artists: David Ashby 25; Martin Camm 21, 22, 23; John Hutchinson 4, 6, 10; Deborah Johnson 20; Ann Savage 24; Paul Williams 18
Maps: AND Map Graphics Ltd.
Photographs: Robert Francis 5 (bottom); 6, 13 (top), 18, 21 (bottom), 25, 26 (top), 27 (top and bottom left); Robert Harding Picture Library 10, 11, 16 (top), 19 (bottom), 21 (left), 22, 23, 24, 28 (bottom); Hutchison Picture Library 1, 3, 5 (top), 7 (bottom), 9, 11 (bottom), 12, 13 (bottom), 14, 17, 19, 28 (top), 29 (top left); Panos 7 (top), 9 (bottom), 16 (bottom), 29 (bottom); Pictor 8 (top left), 15 (top), 26 (bottom); Travel Ink 27 (right), 29 (top right).
All other photographs by Digital Stock and Digital Vision.

Cataloging-in-publication data

Morris, Neil
        Rivers and lakes / Neil Morris
p. cm. — (The wonders of our world)
Includes index.
ISBN 0-86505-834-2 (library bound) ISBN 0-86505-846-6 (pbk.)
Summary: Examines rivers and lakes of the world, discussing the different types, their histories, wildlife, and effects on humans.
1. Rivers—Juvenile literature. 2. Lakes—Juvenile literature.
[1. Rivers. 2. Lakes.] I. Title. II. Series: Morris, Neil. Wonders of our world.

GB1203.8.M673 1998   j551.48'3   LC 98-11202 CIP

E
551.48
Mor
c.2

© 1998 Crabtree Publishing Company
Created and produced by Snapdragon Publishing Ltd. in conjunction with Crabtree Publishing Company.

Without limiting the rights under copyright reserved above, no part of this publication may be reproduced, stored in or introduced into a retrieval system, or transmitted, in any form or by any means (electronic, mechanical, photocopying, recording or otherwise) without the prior permission of the publisher of this book.

CONTENTS

WHAT IS A RIVER?

A RIVER is a large natural course of fresh water that flows in a channel. Most rivers start as small streams high up on hills and mountains. When rain falls on high land, some of it seeps into the ground. Some water, however, stays on the surface and flows downhill in streams.

Further on, streams join to make a small river. Small rivers join to make one big, wide river. Rivers flow downhill across the land until they reach the sea.

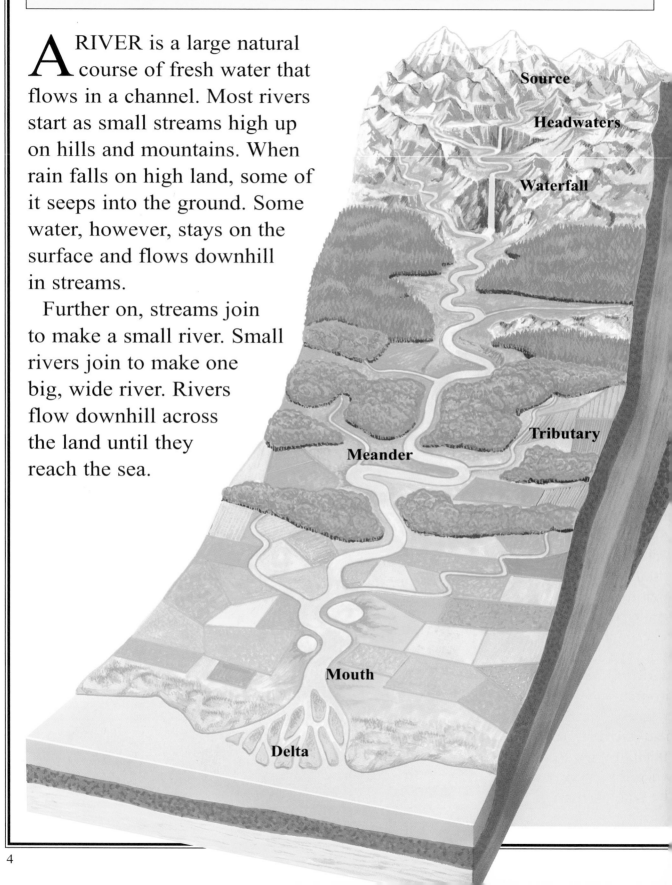

Source

Headwaters

Waterfall

Tributary

Meander

Mouth

Delta

HEADWATERS

Many small streams flow together to form the headwaters of a river. Here the water is usually shallow and fast-moving (above). As it tumbles down steep slopes, the falling water wears away the land and carries with it grit and rocks.

GANGES DELTA

When they get near the sea, some big rivers split into many smaller channels and form a delta. The delta of the Ganges River (above), in Bangladesh, is the world's biggest.

FROM SOURCE TO MOUTH

The beginning of a river is called its source. In high, cold regions, the water at the source often comes from melting snow and ice. When the river reaches flatter land, it gets wider and starts to loop around, making meanders, or bends. The river ends at its mouth, the place where it flows into the sea.

TRIBUTARY

A SMALL river that flows into a larger one is called a tributary.

The photograph below shows a narrow tributary at the point where it joins the East Alligator River, in northern Australia.

WHAT IS A LAKE?

A LAKE IS a body of water that is surrounded by land. Lakes form in hollows in the earth's surface, called basins. Their water comes from rainfall or melting snow, and much of it flows in from small streams or rivers. Most lakes are full of fresh water and have at least one river flowing out.

Many lake basins were made a long time ago by glaciers. Others formed when forces inside the earth made its surface move or crack.

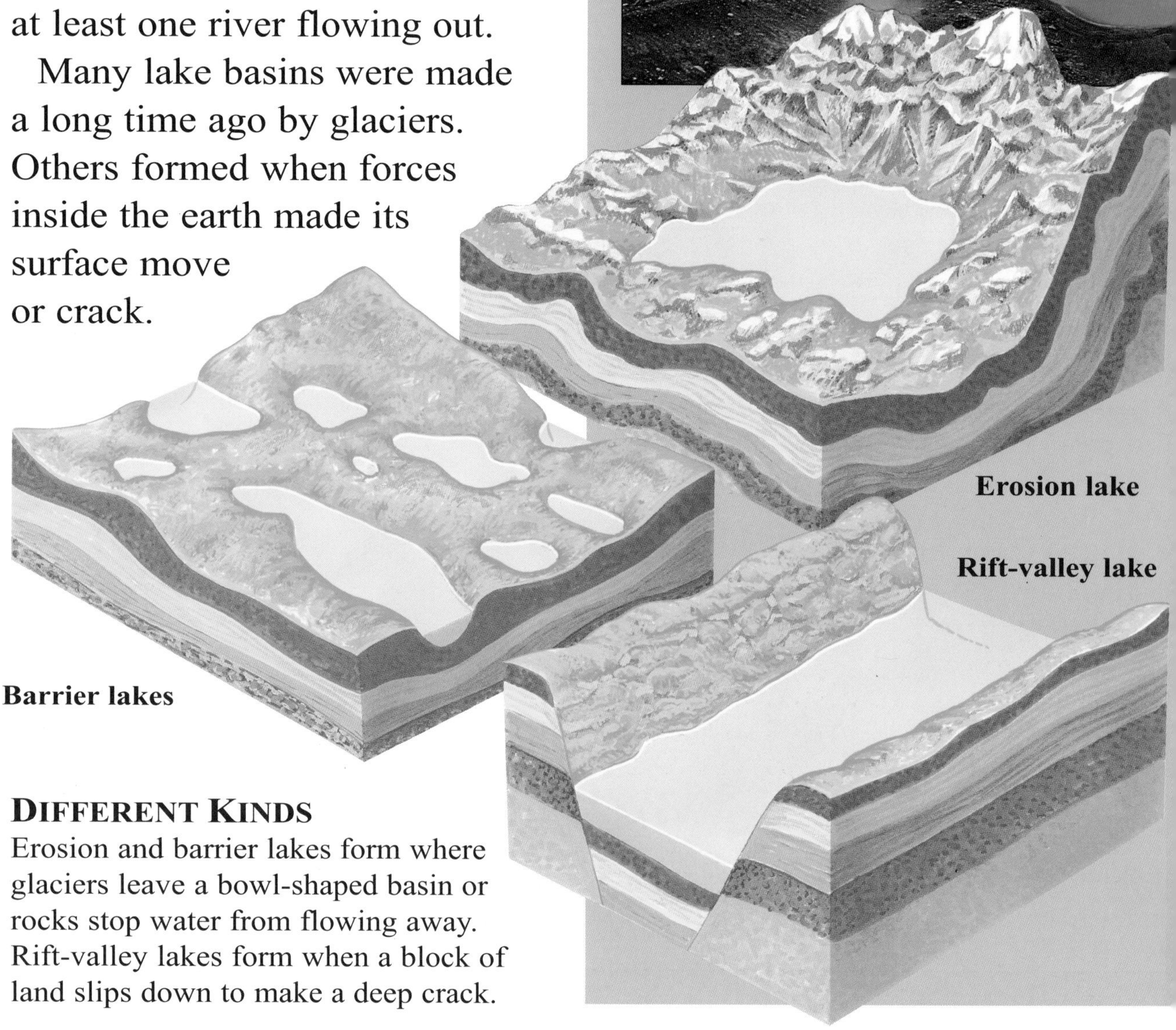

Erosion lake

Rift-valley lake

Barrier lakes

DIFFERENT KINDS

Erosion and barrier lakes form where glaciers leave a bowl-shaped basin or rocks stop water from flowing away. Rift-valley lakes form when a block of land slips down to make a deep crack.

WORLD'S DEEPEST LAKE

LAKE Baikal, in eastern Russia, is 5,315 feet (1 620 meters) at its deepest point. This rift-valley lake holds more than a fifth of the world's fresh water. It has 336 rivers flowing into it, but just one flowing out. The lake's surface freezes over each winter.

VOLCANIC LAKE

Lakes also form when rain and melting snow fill the craters of volcanoes. Mount Tongariro (above), in New Zealand, has big and small crater lakes.

CASPIAN SEA

THE Caspian Sea, a salt-water lake between Europe and Asia, is the biggest lake in the world. Its surface area of 143,250 square miles (371 000 square kilometers) makes it even larger than the five Great Lakes added together.

WHERE IN THE WORLD?

THERE ARE rivers and lakes on all the world's continents except Antarctica. Rivers have many tributaries. Each tributary has a different source and, usually, a different name. A river's length is measured from the source that is farthest from its mouth.

Many of the world's biggest lakes are in North America. Large lakes are also found in eastern Africa, along the Great Rift Valley. The Great Rift Valley is made up of faults in the earth's surface, caused by earthquakes millions of years ago.

WHERE ARE THEY?
This map shows the location of the world's ten longest rivers and ten biggest lakes.

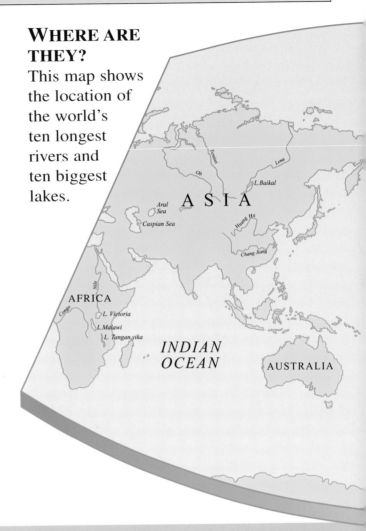

AMAZON RIVER
The second-longest river in the world, the Amazon (left), carries more water than any other. It is made up of over a fifth of all the water in the world's rivers. Its source is high in the Andes mountains of Peru. It flows across the plains of Brazil, through a vast rainforest, to the Atlantic Ocean.

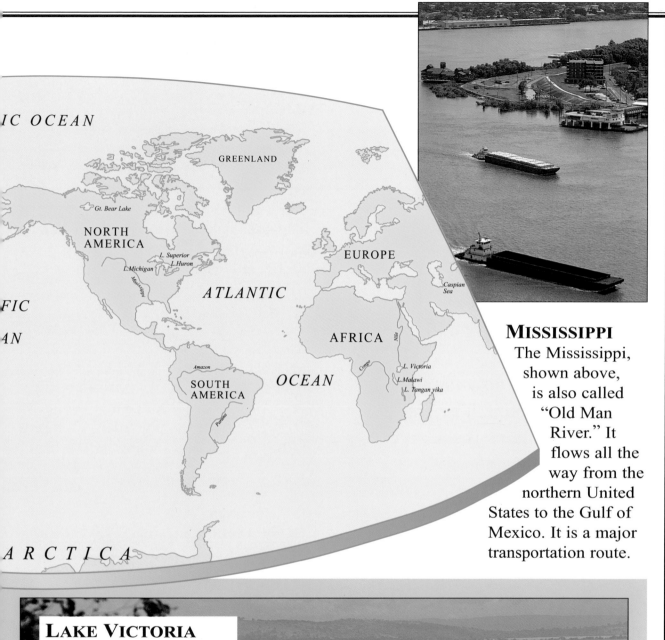

MISSISSIPPI

The Mississippi, shown above, is also called "Old Man River." It flows all the way from the northern United States to the Gulf of Mexico. It is a major transportation route.

LAKE VICTORIA

AFRICA'S largest lake, Victoria, lies 3,723 feet (1 135 meters) above sea level. It sits on a high plateau between two rift valleys. The Victoria Nile, a tributary of the Nile River, is the only river that flows out of Lake Victoria.

WATER ON THE MOVE

MOST RIVERS flow year-round. As it flows, a river wears away the land and cuts a channel into the ground. Its water carries along some of the soil and stones the river has worn away. This moving load scrapes against the river's bed and banks, making an even deeper, wider channel for the water.

A river drains rainwater from the land around it. The land that a river drains is the river's drainage basin.

THE WATER CYCLE

Water moves in a never-ending cycle (below). The sun's heat changes some of the water in oceans and on the land into vapor. Water vapor rises into the air and then cools to form droplets of water. The droplets join together to make clouds, and later fall back to earth as rain. Some of this rainwater forms rivers and lakes. Rivers take water back to the ocean, and then the water cycle starts all over again.

FISHING RAPIDS

PEOPLE in the African country of Congo fish in the Zaire River's rapids (right), where shallow water rushes over rocks.

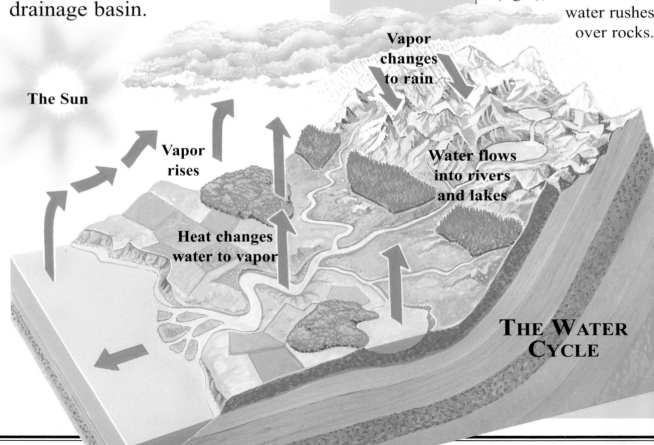

The Sun

Vapor rises

Heat changes water to vapor

Vapor changes to rain

Water flows into rivers and lakes

THE WATER CYCLE

GRAND CANYON

It has taken millions of years for the Colorado River to carve the Grand Canyon in Arizona, USA (above). This enormous gorge drops away to a depth of one mile (1.6 kilometers).

NIAGARA FALLS

Halfway between Lakes Erie and Ontario, on the Canada-USA border, the Niagara River plunges about 176 feet (54 meters) over a steep gorge. Niagara's two waterfalls, shown below, are world-famous.

LONGEST RIVER

THE NILE is the longest river in the world. It flows 4,145 miles (6 670 kilometers), from its source in central Africa to its mouth on the Mediterranean Sea. The river has two branches. They are called the White Nile and Blue Nile because of the different colors of their waters.

The farthest tributary of the White Nile starts in Burundi, flows into Lake Victoria, and heads north. At Khartoum it joins the Blue Nile. The Nile River brings life to the desert countries of Sudan and Egypt.

WATERING THE DESERT

SOME farming techniques have been used in Egypt for thousands of years. The man above lifts water from a canal with a traditional device called a shaduf. Canals and ditches help take the Nile's water to fields.

WILD WATER

LIKE all big rivers, the Nile has many tributaries with fast and rocky head-waters. Ugandan women, shown left, use the wild water of a White Nile tributary to do their washing. The Blue Nile, which flows even faster, rises in the highlands of Ethiopia.

CAPITAL ON THE NILE

Cairo, shown above, the capital city of Egypt, lies on the banks of the Nile. The city was founded over a thousand years ago, near the famous pyramids of Giza. The ancient Egyptians fished and bathed in the Nile, drank its waters, and worshiped it for spreading fertile mud over the land when it flooded each year.

ASWAN

The city of Aswan is on the east bank of the Nile, south of Cairo. At the edge of the city (below), the desert comes almost to the river. Rocks from Aswan were used to build monuments in ancient times. South of the city is the Aswan High Dam, which was built across the Nile to create a steady flow of water year-round.

GREAT LAKES

THE FIVE Great Lakes, in North America, are the world's largest group of fresh-water lakes. They formed when the glaciers that covered the region many thousands of years ago melted. Water filled the basins dug out by the glaciers.

Canada and the United States share four of the lakes including the largest, Lake Superior. Lake Michigan is in the United States. Together, the five Great Lakes form part of an enormous inland waterway.

ST. LAWRENCE SEAWAY

THE St. Lawrence Seaway (above) links the Great Lakes to the Atlantic Ocean. A series of canals and locks allows ships to sail over 2,300 miles (3,700 kilometers) from the Atlantic to the port of Duluth, Minnesota. Ships load up at ports such as Sarnia, Ontario (below), on the St. Clair River.

LARGEST GREAT LAKE

Lake Superior is the world's largest fresh-water lake. It is also the deepest of the Great Lakes, and the highest – it lies at 600 feet (183 meters) above sea level.

The rocks and forests of the Apostle Islands (above), in Lake Superior, are part of a protected US National Lakeshore. Snowshoe hares, beavers, and foxes live on the lake's largest island, Isle Royale.

LAKESIDE CITY

THE city of Chicago, USA, is built on the shores of Lake Michigan (below). It has some of the world's tallest buildings. The city is divided by the Chicago River, which today flows away from the lake. In 1900, engineers built canals to reverse the river's flow, to stop sewage from entering the lake.

FLOODS

ALMOST ALL rivers flood from time to time, usually when there is much more rain than usual. When this happens, a river rises above its normal level and overflows its banks.

People in areas threatened by floods use rock, soil and sandbags to build levees. These may hold back rising water, but do not stop floods further downstream. This happens regularly to the Huang He River in China, where, over the centuries, millions of people have been killed by floods. Because of this, the river is often called "China's sorrow."

MISSISSIPPI DISASTER

In 1993, the Mississippi River flooded and left 74,000 people homeless. The farm above is near Cairo, Illinois, where the Mississippi is joined by the Ohio River and doubles its volume of water.

BANGLADESH

THIS big levee (left), or embankment, was built as a flood defense for Dhaka, the capital of Bangladesh. The city lies on one of the rivers of the Ganges delta, where heavy monsoon rain often causes flooding.

FLOOD DEFENSE

THE Chinese people above are working hard to build up flood defense walls after they were breached by the river. China's longest river, the Chang Jiang, had severe floods in 1995.

CITY FLOODING

Cities may have artificial banks to stop floods, but the rivers still flood. The Seine River (above) has overflowed its banks near the center of Paris, France.

THAMES BARRIER

The Thames Barrier protects London, England, from floods. Raising the gates stops water flowing into the Thames River. The huge "shells" below cover the machinery that controls the gates.

WATER POWER

BY BUILDING dams across rivers, people use the power of rushing water to make electricity. This energy is called hydroelectricity. The first water-powered plant for generating electricity was built in the United States in 1882. Since then, dams have become bigger and plants more powerful.

Controlling rivers in this way brings problems as well as benefits. Dams change a river's natural course and create huge reservoirs, or lakes, that cover useful land.

GENERATING ELECTRICITY

THE power plant on the Snowy River (above), in Australia, is part of a hydroelectric network. Dams build up huge amounts of water in a reservoir (below). As the water rushes through a penstock, or channel, it turns the blades of a turbine that drives a generator. This produces electricity, which is sent over power lines to factories and homes.

BUILDING A DAM

Building the huge Itaipu dam (above), on the Paraná River between Brazil and Paraguay, took 17 years, and employed 40,000 construction workers.

GLEN CANYON

The Glen Canyon dam (below) is built across the Colorado River, in Arizona, USA, at the edge of the Grand Canyon. It is 710 feet (216 meters) high.

EGYPTIAN TREASURES

THE Great Temple of Rameses II (above) is over 3,000 years old. When the Aswan High Dam was built across the Nile, the temple would have been flooded by the dam's reservoir. It was cut into blocks, moved, and rebuilt 200 feet (60 meters) higher up.

ANIMALS

RIVERS AND lakes are home to many kinds of insects, birds, and amphibians, as well as some mammals and reptiles. Few plants survive in the fast-flowing upper waters of a river, so there is little for animals to feed on. In areas where the river is slower and wider, plants grow on the river bed and on its banks.

In the still waters of lakes, tiny plants grow quickly, providing food for many small animals. These in turn become food for other larger animals.

FRESHWATER SEAL

The world's smallest seal (right) lives in the cold waters of Lake Baikal, in Russia. The lake contains many fish, as well as a third of the world's freshwater shrimps, so there is plenty for the Baikal seals to feed on. New factories around the shores of the lake, however, are polluting the seals' habitat.

BEAVER DAMS

Beavers (above, left) gnaw through tree trunks and build dams to make still, safe ponds. There they build their lodges of sticks and mud.

Amazon **Chiang Jiang** **Ganges**

RIVER DOLPHINS

MOST dolphins swim in salty oceans, but there are freshwater species (above) in three big rivers. They all have long, slender beaks and poor eyesight. They find their way around by sending out high-pitched sounds that bounce off things and make an echo. All these dolphins are in danger of becoming extinct.

MUTE SWANS
Swans feed mainly on underwater plants, which they reach easily with their long necks. Mute swans (above) nest on rivers and lakes in northern Europe and Asia. Mute means "silent." Mute swans are quieter than others, but they hiss if threatened. Young swans, or cygnets, have gray feathers.

ESTUARINE CROCODILE

THE estuarine crocodile (below) lives in estuaries, the wide part of rivers near their mouth, where fresh water mixes with salty sea water. The crocodile below is making its way through the soft mud of an Australian estuary. These large reptiles can grow up to 19 feet (6 meters) long, and spend little time on land. Females lay their eggs in mounds of plant material.

FISH

THERE ARE fish in most of the world's rivers and lakes. Some, such as graylings and some trout, like clear, fast-moving rivers. Others, such as carp and catfish, live in muddy, slow-flowing rivers.

Lakes are home to other kinds of fish, such as perch and some kinds of bass. Many lake fish live near the surface in summer. In winter, however, if the surface of the lake freezes, they move away from the ice, down to deeper water.

LAKE DWELLERS

THE lake trout above has an unwelcome guest, a bloodsucking sea lamprey. Lampreys swim into the Great Lakes from the Atlantic Ocean and feed on fish, which then may die.

PIRANHA

PIRANHAS live in rivers and lakes in South America. They have strong jaws and razor-sharp teeth (left) and feed on other fish, as well as seeds or fruit. Piranhas are only about 12 inches (30 centimeters) long, but they often hunt in schools, attacking and tearing apart large animals.

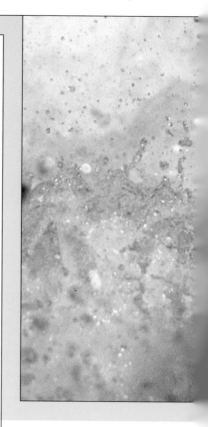

Nile perch

Tropical cichlid

PREDATOR AND PREY

FISH flourish where there are few predators to hunt them. In Lake Victoria, for example, there are hundreds of different kinds of small tropical fish, including the cichlid (above). In 1964, people put Nile perch (above) into the lake so that there would be larger fish to catch. Since then, this predator has killed off many of the smaller fish.

SWIMMING UPSTREAM

Salmon spend most of their lives swimming in the ocean. Then they return to their home river or stream to spawn, sometimes traveling as far as 2,000 miles (3 200 kilometers). These sockeye salmon (left) have swam from the Pacific Ocean and are leaping up a fast-flowing river in Alaska, USA. The journey of the salmon becomes harder as they near the river's rushing headwaters.

LAKE PEOPLE

Many ancient civilizations grew up near lakes or in river valleys. In these places, people were close to the water they needed to survive. The Sumerians, for example, lived between the Tigris and Euphrates Rivers in southwest Asia, and the Egyptians along the Nile River in Africa.

As well as water, rivers and lakes provide fish for food. Transport is often easier by boat than overland.

CELTIC SETTLEMENT

Over 2,500 years ago, there was a large Celtic settlement near the modern lakeside town of Hallstatt (below, left), in Austria. There the Celts mined salt, traded, and made things in bronze and iron. The small bronze figure (below, right) shows how Celts dressed.

LAND IN A LAKE

ABOUT 700 years ago, the Aztecs built a village on a marshy island in a Mexican lake. To make the island bigger, they dredged mud from the bottom of the shallow lake and built reed platforms. The village became a city, which was later destroyed by Spanish invaders. Modern Mexico City is built on its ruins.

BATAK PEOPLE
The Batak people live by Lake Toba, a crater lake on the Indonesian island of Sumatra. The Batak woman shown right holds a fish that was farmed in the lake.

PEOPLE OF TITICACA
Lake Titicaca lies high in the Andes mountains, on the Peru-Bolivia border. Its shores (above) are home to the Aymara people. They traditionally use the reeds that grow around the lake to make huts and boats.

RIVERS AND lakes, and the reservoirs connected to them, provide all of us with water. They are also important for transportation. Today, as in the distant past, heavy goods are carried by barges along the world's waterways. Ferries are common on the bigger lakes and rivers. People also sail and row boats for pleasure, and tourists take cruises on scenic and historic routes. Fishing with nets is an important industry, especially in big lakes, and angling with rods is a popular sport.

ANGLING FOR FUN
Many anglers fish purely for sport, putting back all they catch. The angler above stands in the Yellowstone River, a tributary of the Missouri in the northwest USA.

DEAD SEA SALT

THE Dead Sea, on the border between Jordan and Israel, is the saltiest lake in the world. It is called "dead" because no fish can live in its waters. Its surface is also the lowest point on the earth's surface, 1,310 feet (399 meters) below sea level. Bathers (above) can float easily in the salty water. Salt (below) and other minerals are extracted from the lake.

TRAFFIC ON THE RHINE

A barge carries goods and a ferry takes tourists along the Rhine River in Germany (left), an important European waterway. The Rhine rises in the Swiss Alps and flows for 820 miles (1320 kilometres) before reaching the North Sea. In 1992, a canal was opened to connect the Main River, a Rhine tributary, to the Danube River, forming a water route from the Black Sea to the North Sea.

WINDSURFING

Lakes are very popular for windsurfing and all forms of sailing. Just like sea coasts, the shores of many lakes have become tourist resorts, with facilities for windsurfers, sailors, and water-skiers.

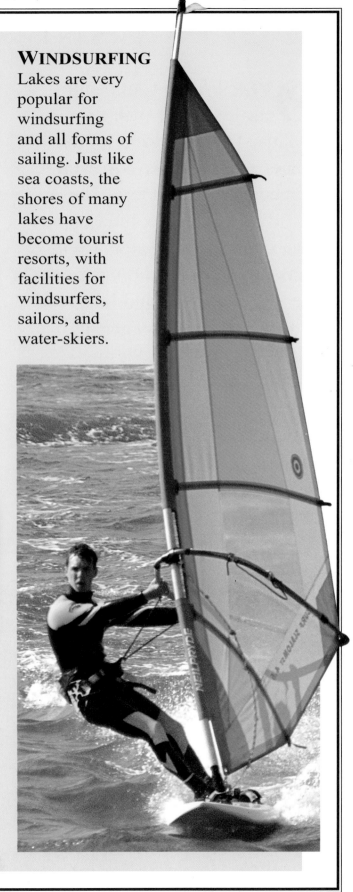

TODAY AND TOMORROW

OVER 90 per cent of the earth's water is in the oceans. Three-quarters of our planet's fresh water is frozen in icecaps and glaciers. The world's largest lake, the Caspian Sea, contains saltwater. These facts highlight just how precious the world's rivers and lakes are to us as sources of water.

It is easy to spoil the world's natural wonders. Industry and tourism make more and more demands on water resources. We must all take care to preserve the beauty and value of our rivers and lakes.

INDUSTRIAL POLLUTION

Many industries need vast quantities of water. That is why factories are often located near rivers and lakes, like the one above, on the East River in New York City. Governments have had to make laws to stop factories that dump waste into rivers.

HOLY RIVER

THE Ganges River is holy to followers of the Hindu religion. Every year, about a million Hindus go to the Indian city of Varanasi (left) to bathe in the river. About 200 million people live in the river's valley, and the river's pollution is a danger to them.

NATIONAL PARK

ENGLAND'S Lake District is a scenic area of lakes and hills. It is a major tourist attraction, with 12 million visitors each year. The area is now protected as a national park.

SHRINKING LAKE

The Aral Sea, in central Asia, is getting smaller. Water from the rivers that feed this salt-water lake has been diverted into irrigation canals. The shoreline has shrunk, leaving boats stranded (left).

THE THREE GORGES DAM

The world's biggest dam is being built on the Chang Jiang River, in China (right). When it opens in 2009, the dam will be the world's most powerful hydro-electric plant. The huge reservoir behind the dam will flood many cities, and 2 million people will have to move.

GLOSSARY

Barrier lake	A lake that has formed where rocks have built up to stop the water from flowing away
Basin	A hollow in the earth's surface, where a lake forms
Canal	An artificial waterway
Continent	One of the earth's seven huge land masses
Crater	A bowl-shaped basin at the top of a volcano
Crust	The hard outer layer of the earth
Delta	A fan-shaped area at the mouth of some rivers, where the river splits into many smaller channels
Drainage basin	An area of land from which a river drains the rainwater
Dredge	To scoop up mud and stones from the bottom of a river or lake
Erosion lake	A lake, in a bowl-shaped basin worn away by a glacier
Estuary	The wide part of a river near its mouth, where the river's fresh water mixes with salty water from the sea
Fault	A crack in the earth's surface
Fertile	Describing land that produces good crops
Glacier	A slowly moving mass of ice
Gorge	A deep ravine
Hydroelectricity	Electricity that is made by water-driven turbines
Ice cap	A thick mass of ice that covers an area of land
Levee	An embankment built to stop a river from flooding

Lock	A part of a canal or river that is closed off by gates. The water level in a lock can be changed. A lock is used to raise and lower the ships that are traveling through it.
Meander	A curve or bend in a river
Mouth	The place where a river flows into the sea
Penstock	A water channel that leads from the wall of a dam to a turbine
Plateau	An area of flat, high land
Pollution	Harmful substances that damage the air, water, or soil
Predator	An animal that hunts other animals for food
Rainforest	A thick forest found in very warm, wet tropical regions
Rapids	A part of a river where water moves very fast over rocks
Reservoir	An artificial lake used to collect and store water
Rift valley	A steep-sided valley formed by land that slips down between cracks in the earth's surface
Rift-valley lake	A lake, found in a deep crack that was formed when a block of land slipped down between cracks in the earth's surface
Sewage	Human waste
Shaduf	A pole, used for raising water, with a bucket at one end and a weight at the other
Source	The place where a river begins
Tributary	A small river that flows into a larger one
Turbine	A machine with blades that are turned by moving water

INDEX

South Branch Library
P.O. Box 96
Breckenridge, Colorado 80424

1 2 3 4 5 6 7 8 9 0 Printed in the U.S.A. 7 6 5 4 3 2 1 0 9 8